FLEEING ACTIUM

Books by Ricardo Pau-Llosa

Sorting Metaphors
Bread of the Imagined
Cuba
Vereda Tropical
The Mastery Impulse
Parable Hunter
Man
The Turning
Fleeing Actium

FLEEING ACTIUM

Ricardo Pau-Llosa

Carnegie Mellon University Press
Pittsburgh 2023

Acknowledgments

Grateful acknowledgment is made of the magazines in which these poems first appeared:

Ambit: "Swimming Pigs". *The American Journal of Poetry*: "Hiroshige, Ōiso"; "Hiroshige, *Kanaya*"; "Ogata Kōrin, *Red and White Plum Blossoms* (c. 1714)"; "The Mystery of Immediacy"; "Dido to Solomon"; "Solomon to Dido"; "Homer to Moses"; "Moses to Homer"; "Husserlian Meditation: Torch Lighter"; "Husserlian Meditation: Ringtone"; "Husserlian Meditation: Thumb Drive"; "View from My Mother's Last Hospital Room"; "Key Largo, Nightfall"; "Cognate, Port Largo"; "Cytokine Storm, The Croc in Plague Time". *Arion*: "Helen to Bathsheba"; "Bathsheba to Helen"; "Jonathan to Patroclus"; "Patroclus to Jonathan"; "Barracks"; "Proteus"; "Puddle". *Bayou*: "Husserlian Meditation: Remote". *Birmingham Poetry Review*: "Stanley Spencer, *Christ in the Wilderness: The Hen* (1954)"; "The Five Senses (series)"; "Hiroshige, *Okabe*"; "Blanket Warmer"; "Katsushika Ōi, *Night Scene in the Yoshiwara* (1850)"; "Office"; "The Lost Sermons of the Buddha (series)"; "Soon". *Blackbird*: "Coming Home"; "Syncretism". *Bombay Review*: "Never Tiger"; "Aubade". *Briar Cliff Review*: "Manta". *Burnside Review*: "Yemayá". *Chariton Review*: "Eres débil". *Clackamas Literary Review*: "Il Principe Ignoto"; "Husserlian Meditation: Truck Tires"; "Homage to Telesilla of Argos (fl. 500 bce), Port Largo"; "Window on the Sea". *Colorado Review*: "Scarpia". *The Common*: "Scarpia (Aside)"; "Nocturne"; "Car Wash, Key Largo". *Crazyhorse*: "Turandot non esiste". *Dalhousie Review*: "Hokusai, *Sparrow Dance* (1815)"; "*Nessun dorma*". *december*: "Tsukioka Yoshitoshi, *Cooling off at Shijō*"; "Leda to Mary"; "Mary to Leda"; "Fleeing Actium". *Ekphrasis*: "The Mummifier's Mummy"; "Eduardo Chillida, *Peine del Viento* (1976)"; "Rio de Janeiro"; "Akashic Field"; "Julio Larraz, *Ice, and Space Time* (2015)"; "Arnaldo Pomodoro, *La Sfera Grande* (1998), Pesaro"; "Clyfford Still, PH-247 (1951)"; "Hokusai, *The Dream of the Fisherman's Wife* (1814)"; "Daruma"; "Hiroshige, *Shinagawa*". *Epoch*: "Tortoise Shell". *Folio*: "The Last Quarter of the 20th Century in Miami". *Hollins Critic*: "Snake". *Hotel Amerika*: "Tawaraya Sōtatsu, *Waves at Matsushima* (1620)"; "Scarpia (a Cavaradossi)". *The Hudson Review*: "Kalypso to Paul of Tarsus". *Ilanot Review*: "Paraíso, Summer"; "Designated Smoking Area". *Interim*: "Husserlian Meditation: Sunday Rain". *Plume*: "Christopher Wood, *Building the Boat, Tréboul* (1930)"; "Willem Van de Velde the Younger, *Ships in a Gale* (1660)"; "Matsumura Goshun, *Crab* (late 18th century)". *Poetry Salzburg Review*: "Hurricane Warning". *PRISM International*: "Husserlian Meditation: Barcode". *Quadrant*: "Hiroshige, *Kanagawa*"; "Garden"; "Balcony, Truman Street, Key West". *Reed*: "Husserlian Meditation: Expiration Dates". *Salamander*: "Echo". *San Pedro River Review*: "Dreamers"; "Night Garden". *Saranac Review*: "Alexander Calder, *Flamingo* (1973–74)"; "Resort". *The Secular Heretic*: "Epistemology at Aleida's Swimming Pool"; "Al Andalus". *Stand*: "Tawaraya Sōtatsu, *Poems of the 36 Immortal Poets over a Painting of Cranes* (c. 1600)"; "Hiroshige, *Morning View at Nihonbashi Bridge*"; "Hiroshige, *Kyobashi Bridge and Bamboo Yards*"; "Gates"; "Shutter Fauna"; "Call". *Vayavya*: "CT Scan"; "Oneiromancy"; "Feeder"

Book design by Jess Jones

Library of Congress Control Number 2023933213
ISBN 978-0-88748-694-4

10 9 8 7 6 5 4 3 2 1

for Aleida

Contents

Ekphrasis

Edo

Belief

Res

Genius loci

The Lost Sermons of the Buddha

Res

Genius loci

EKPHRASIS

The Mummifier's Mummy

Like the tailor's suit or the chef's meal, simplicity
signals the master. No coifs or vivid tinctures
brow the face that studied death, sure
in his craft. A clutched, worn tool, for humility
beneath the stitched rictus of his vesseled
prayer. A pupil perhaps, or a rival, performed
this task and, honoring what the master scorned,
urned him basely. With him terse was sealed
the knowledge of what little hope there is
in ritual—that private magic that makes symbols
of things. Neither can we extract balms
from edicts that Illusion, by reason, is all that is.
Even shadows lunge at this leathered state,
crouched in clay, pretending no better fate.

Eduardo Chillida, *Peine del Viento* (1976)

Identity theft for crabs
creviced amid detonating waves.
Claws know themselves plagiarized,
their surgical tweezers which floods
of centuries designed, stabbed
into a granite herd, grasping
the spirit tumbling, uncombed.
A chorus fury, then still-shot of somnambulance.
The prongs stare more than seize
to pry themselves from nature's
thrown dice, mark resentment
of toil, furnace, plow.
Such fists affirm there is no life
but on anvils. Rocks endure
the singularities of waves. Sailors
could mock these deformed dock cleats
or metal that bent outlived a vessel fire,
like the remains of Caligula's barges.
History wars against itself. Such hunters
of the bleak familiar forget
that eons tell how some labor here
for wind and others for salt.

Christopher Wood, *Building the Boat, Trèboul* (1930)

Halfway, the basket nature of the ship
reveals itself, to us though not perhaps
to the two men or the women bringing material
or sitting in gossip on the quay, for, though real
enough to place the setting—Normandy,
let's say—the quotidian, like drama, demands
the craned neck of symbolism and not just
the calm chew of experience. Meaning trusts
variables, as if any sequel of actions
and jot of causes, accidents, and apprehensions
which converge into an event—a temporal
thing free from the things in it, the moral
and aesthetic, even the tangled beings involved—
yearned for the fill of horizons. A puzzle is solved
when it can sustain, like a bulging sail, multiple
endings, all equally true and loyal
to the root of mystery. The ship, then, is a basket
on the still life of the dock, a cradle, though not a casket,
for who builds his own rocking end joyous
with the sweat of labor? The ribbed beams, yes,
are skeletal, and the side planks presage the shells
we hide in to face the world. But the swells
this vessel will ride, and the bolt and shadow
that frees the molten sea from the syllogism of meadow
and valley, tell us there is no thing or process
that doesn't envy art's prism of choices.

Alexander Calder, *Flamingo* (1973-74)

Most nervous of lanky birds
yet icon of elegant patience.
Forever sifting the concrete waters
for critters too small to mourn.
Whalers slaughtering
or hunters mounding inedible
horns merit our disgust,
but not nature's methodical
harvester. Cold unfelt data
is hunger's kiln; we ponder
in arm-crossed hum. At times
hearts chasten apart the pride
killing the giraffe colt
or the vulture squadron
cleaning the beach
of turtle hatchlings. Should
we knight forth to save
the insolvent brood? Flamingo,
rhea, ostrich faced a 19th century
of ravenous fashion. Now
the giant steel sculpture
blushes among virile introvert
panes, bronze jawed
grids that universal mask
the minds of colossi.
Beauty drenches the otherwise desert,
homages wading and abrupt lift
into pink fire. The clouds rattle
with fake dawn. Such dance and flight
mate our freedoms with delicate beasts
in dream's anchor images.
This soldiers know:
a cannonball too is the child
of arc and flame.

Rio de Janeiro

after the photograph by Marc Ferrez

"Ent'ring with cheerful shouts the wat'ry reign, . . ."
          Aeneid, Bk I, (Dryden tr.)

That distance is a sea
is confirmed by the photograph.
The 19th-century view
shows the foreground
in harvest nearness
of coral plenaries,
the raucous details sharpened
by what should have veiled.
The mid-ground calms
in the discourse of apparition,
a cetacean lumber,
neither still nor agile.

It is here that Ferrez
breached his Guanabara whales
and netted the shoal
of particulars that grasp as city.
Beyond are the myriads
whose pages we close
into the book of far.
Yet wordy are its realms
of definition
between horizon crests
culled into the sleep of clouds
and that sleep.
So like the ocean
is our sense of space
that it is hard to tell

the model from the clarity.
Landscape edges into depths,
and sea machineries
in their opaque roll invest
the mind in dune and chasm.

It could not be any other way
if we are to behold on sheets
the theft of image
once carried by a beam,
wrecked upon the glassy shore
and made to tell the ardent tale
of how the ocean taught us
how to see, and why
our mount of details can only keel
upon the pages of a fiery reef.

Akashic Field

after the painting *Philosopher's Stone* by Melvin Martínez

A book's Borgesian fate is to ape the universe,
letter upon word upon sentence upon page upon tomes,
shelves upon stacks upon floors, all compressed
into a dot, a sparkle that prisms a beam that roams

from sun to cliff to lake to turbine to electrical
net, allowing a night reader to illuminate.
But the painting makes quite a different call.
Vapor as muse defines the indeterminate

flesh of all form, dissolves even
as it edges, smudges the rectilinear embrace
with bejeweled beguilings, tidal pools of broken
reflections that reveal how science now can trace

the journey of light from matter to purity and back.
Veils map the dancer's urgent track.

Stanley Spencer, *Christ in the Wilderness: The Hen* (1954)

The implication is he is the mountains
guarding the stubborn city, that hen and its chicks
he dreams of resembling. He always speaks
in metaphor, so that his similes retain

the unifying alchemy of the verb *Be.*
Truth is, the chicks will follow anything
that promises cover, or invites a shallow worshipping.
Soon the idols will be replaced by

bad troubadors and doped acrobats,
and the golden hen will wait still poor
for future's company, dumb and inured
to undeservedness. The rattle of caveats

will not deter the silent man of mountains.
Not speaker but word. Like wind, the refrain.

Julio Larraz, *Ice, and Space Time* (2015)

Vapor, too, is present, always, ghost
shocking yet boredom's ubiquity.
The block of ice ignites our view of lost
fires, blue infernos. Ice is the frailty

that gulps a sea, masks and unmasks
the noon of fallen fruit. These lumber like dice
and catch us catching them in the mercurial flask
of spilled mirror, angled by the sun the ice

has paved onto the stage. The frigid stare
pages and wombs the warps with which the mind
consoles us in this drowning clock. No rest
in sea or block, nor in bled silvers, nor in rind

or spheres—nothing but what escapes the scene
into the aria of light from matter's scheme.

Coming Home

after various paintings by Julio Larraz

The fruit pile up impossibly, a balance
that is unbalanced to desire, aping a truck
of clouds shoveled by weather into bulk
like luggage rubbled on the carousel

haloed by passengers still waiting for their bags.
Light, too, has grown greedy with patience.
It lurks on the domed roof of the pale house
atop the bone and olive escarpment. It magmas

in the arena's gut, burps in the irate cloud.
Tired of fencing the track of the temporal race,
of being the needle that minds the universe,
it warms the nested sigh of the thickening mound.

Comforting that light is also languor driven.
Though waking with us, it denies we're kin.

Arnaldo Pomodoro, *La Sfera Grande* (1998), Pesaro

It cannot know itself, reflected
on the biting ripples, for though it globes
the eye, it blossoms into machine.
Flayed yet holding its spherical,
it tilts to flirt with axis and season.
Quotes what unshells to reveal and spawn,
yet it cannot be found in nature
or man alone, this orb of concentric hungers,
clock mazed. Quotes myth—the golden
apple of querulous thighs—yet it cannot
tabernacle, nor is it a state palm-warmed
lest crown fails and men must scurry
into sense and laws. It rolls
along the horizon it spun
from its gut, a spider's egg,
a knot in sheets on which
a prisoner climbs to freedom.
A closing book is a breached sphere.

Willem Van de Velde the Younger, *Ships in a Gale* (1660)

The storm dissolves the difference between wave,
rock, and plank, which calm asserts.
The ships seem doomed, masts tilting, naves
rattled, the brink life always is
set in bleakness cinema. An outcrop of granite
that smashed one vessel now gathers
dots of men in crests that just might
toss them to a safe height. An egg's changes
for the moment's fish, but bets are on and winners
will also lose. Time has it, that slippery
boulder. We dryly watch the pummeled swimmers,
tipping hulls, mast climbers whose misery
disciplines valor, and the sea whose beauty is rage,
though history's losses tally on a separate page.

Clyfford Still, PH-247 (1951)

To track and muddy blue is rebel's quarry,
to scribe seasons by meadow clumps and think
not sky or sea, nor lapis. Feel the starry
fate of measure, unsettled yet ample sunk
in clock's parole of rest. The ardent crease,
rip, drip—this orange blood of light
is a nervous tearing infinite that must cease
for us but persists horizoned. And the plinth of night,
the road each shadow spawns, the pour of shut
dreamt forgotten curtain. And a white
edge, the blighted lamb in a rut
disowned, back among us, prodigal and ripe
for seeing what the world of hands has made
of world—this cobalt chant and terminal ode.

The Five Senses

after the series of paintings *The Five Senses* by Jan Brueghel the Elder and Peter Paul Rubens (1617–18)

Hearing

A garden of cochleas compose the scene which eye
dizzies into swirls that lock and free like galaxies.
The chime of clocks and hunting calls demure
asides to mobs of cellos and violins, harpsichord
and talky guests who dine on sound and hoard
the corner where the eye is thrown by the lure
of feast. Plucks and birds circle and seize
Cupid's venison trance as mother rides
the lute which painting cannot record. So deaf
the muted art that theater must fuss bereft
in copious mess to banquet what ear surgeons
clear. Thunder and all its clan and voice
are but ripples which a clutch of bones
and a fluid curl translate into a noise
of chemical and spark. Their journeys end
in luxury's vaulted den, the veiled mind,
whose maze reminds that silence was their origin.

Sight

The cyclopic chandelier ponders the world
of the *mise-en-scène*. It blurs gold with ash
on its brass orb. Pages of visuality surf
upon the paintings within paintings; a mall
of palaces mirrors a hive of art on the wall.
A dozen busts forum the shelves, cursed
with a stone gaze, as lions and men perish
in an orgied hunt. A goddess sits, schooled
in right vision by her son and mired
by wreaths, virgins, lechers. She is too tired
to learn or rage, will shut her eyes and dream
of rest. Conch infinites imploding abound,
for none can take whole this flood of scene,
and must piecemeal build a world in the round.
The eye itself, globe and prism, lets the brain
compose and rectify this detailed rain.
She wonders how each blink a miracle refrains.

Touch

Alone, the sense our bodies own entire.
It warns, detects, gives and pleasure takes.
The hand pulls the resting arm to want,
but all flesh feels the warmth of its brush.
Armor walls from blade, not rush;
it cannot spare us the shot of lure and taunt.
Flesh seals us when, eyes shut, it makes
for sleep. Fearless when we dream of fire.
Ablaze with the silk of oils when entwined,
alone we sank and rise alone to find
we are a crumpled page the dream as author
tossed aside. No such confusion derides
the falcon's prey or the knotted fists the forger
drops and the lasher meticulously plies.
What stroke, note, or pose, what meal or act
was ever free from the body's grip and tact?
This skin that halves the world cannot subtract.

Smell

The floral stampede conflates all scents
into one. No ear or eye, the nose cannot
tell from where or unravel the vines that shape
the clumped aroma. It is false that some detect
by hints the mosaic of waft, for none can reject
the sweep. Rose and jasmine with civet and ape
duel then mate. Behold the dog which forgot
his enemy before him. The goddess sensed
the world could meld and so invented love.
She made the nose her agent, not heart or dove,
not song or sugars bowed, as in Indian lore,
to shoot the guarding will and let trapped
passions roam. A life of thought can no more
quarrel with desire than a nose with odors mobbed.
Like the ear, the nose cannot resist
what enters it. No closing lid desists
nor tongue or hand refuse muddled air's fine grist.

Taste

To eat we kill. Dismiss the chubby shooter
who aims at lust, and fill the room with need's
slaughter. The boar alone manages a severed grin
below the martyred deer and over pheasants
round as bubbles in a drain. None of pleasant's
fineries, the table, field, and floor derange
with pantries or grazing beasts who soon will feed.
The goddess dresses almost right for dinner
as her satyr pours his heart out to allay
whatever haunt of measure might betray
that plenty is not the stuff of paradise.
What then was Eden for, what promise merits
devotion? This vale of no's, this crib that dies
each hour, seeks counterweight in tons not carats,
visions, or wings. The banquet's litany rebuffs
hungers timed to last. Spare us the rough
edge of doubt. We toast sweet pleasure's cuffs.

EDO

Tawaraya Sōtatsu, *Poems of the 36 Immortal Poets over a Painting of Cranes* (c. 1600)

Art resists the destiny of fragility.
Are the cranes, manic as mist in the wind,
the foil to language? Do strokes symptom pity
in their molten lace while flocks pretend

the scrolled horizon cannot truly end?
Transcendence has a cynical accountant
who harps the abacus beads on golden
bars. He wagers on luck against abundant

skill and is nearly right when he's half wrong.
Flight ambiguous, the image is a shell
for the story of how signs drive a throng's
escape on silk. From the painting's well

a treasoned freedom springs. What soars:
the cranes in rebel stream, the words as oars?

Tawaraya Sōtatsu, *Waves at Matsushima* (1620)

"Whether [Devadatta] was cast into hell or not is uncertain,
but he never came back from the swamp!"
—Chittadhar Hridaya, *Sugata Saurabha* [trans. Lewis &
Tuladhar], I:18, Oxford University Press, 2010

The planet scalds with strife, the castled stone
against the gnawing sea, the sword of sun
piercing the moon hush. There is no peace
here, which tempts those failed refugees
of savored despair to head for the heart of the wheel,
rummage tune, and shed the lambent will.
This world defames the temperance of flame,
for no fires assail the snow that tames
Fuji; between mayhems, the gods sleep.
The waves need no tinder sparked to reap
the gravel that once invincibility claimed.
The shore's only order is a fiction framed
by the eye. He walks convinced he is the author
of a burning drowning warring fleeing surrender.

In poured creams of gold Sōtatsu combs
the sea. As hottest flames and metals snow,
the waves trapped in cove and cauldron foam
into teeth. By color they kin the winter show
of mounds, all stillness and deceit,
for nowhere but on silk can a mind sleep
kindly, unadorned with fear. Measures neat
and swirls that shock granite and sky keep
the thunder of some god at bay and lets
the artist's demon rest free contained.
The slash of tidal blades on rock tests
the valiant eye who wonders if, restrained,

a painting masters more the world than one
which races into it, howling wounded hound.

He knew and painted the hells I've borne and live,
for in these depths—thrown from cold to hot,
no future or past—the chained find relief
in timelessness. The ebb and high are caught
in the equal mirrors of the damnèd mind. From here
alone does cause mate with effect and blossom
rot and perfume, slash and caress. The pure
waves of satin tracks that surge with flotsam
procure a stubborn pleasure, a friction of demise
and return. He surely heard my derelict
muse and gathered sea to banner the rise
of light I've earned in darkness. A soul wrecked
will echoes find in art, to grammar misery,
heal expulsion and burn, like incense or memory.

Ogata Kōrin, *Red and White Plum Blossoms* (c. 1714)

Three rivers have I; the curves reveal them,
though only one is brave enough to call
himself a river. Ignore the hero; pretend
he too is mystery. In fact, in all

creation, so few things hide perfectly
from the name we give them. "Tree" is far from sight
though we can touch it, shelter rain and daily
sway from sweat. Getting its bark right

meant dripping paint on wet paint
until a turbulence disclosed its jewel condition.
Then it taught the constant flow constraint.
Blossom, the stream retorted, was the mission

of his desperate brood. They seek the pond of death
and petals where future wrestles them to rest.
The tree took refuge from the aimless swirls
to boast the lineage signed by jagged words

the branches jotted on the golden earth. The infinite
is a language, too, and not the sum of distances.
But river blinded on, a road above an intricate
innocence. And though he mocks dizziness,

each curl foretells the knotted grains a tree
becomes. I fall but am never felled,
his tactile scroll asserts. They then agreed
to be the spirits of the day, time compelled

but moment's rebels. Two seasons will guard
their station in this painting whose mottled trunks
tell half the story and leave to loom the part
where none step twice. Petals in place of husks.

Matsumura Goshun, *Crab*
(late 18th century)

Three frogs and a crab, with a handful of strokes,
and a poem on the side. The paper, too, talks
its abacus of bump and weave. Time drags
itself into the picture through nature and sands

we slander empty. No void in our world
for mind would dab it full, subtle cauldron.
We are the plodding and the scurrying; wet
or dry, aliens of the immediate. No life regret

can bend a body back to what it knew,
so the land crab lugs its armor, stews
in its heat. The frog, sleek and aberrant,
master of the world's two selves, is tenant

and lord. They welcome what new confusions arise
for resignation sometimes gets the prize.

Hokusai, *The Dream of the Fisherman's Wife* (1814)

"O, don't stop," the lone figure
on the edge of a coastal rock says to the wave
that is raking the fish toward him. "Scare more
my way!" Susano-O pities him above
the others who have ships and teams. The poor
man spends days here to stave
off hunger. His young wife endures
the absence and danger, feeds her paltry babes.
Some nights she has a visitor,
bulbous head and fists for eyes. He craves
the taste of her loins. The welcome marauder
lives among them. Some villagers rave
about his skill—a celebrity for a neighbor
in meager Sumida. Art makes him brave
the scandal, for who else could procure
such beauty bereft, sweep them into depraved
habits, and roll them into the endless pure.
He'd give her a print, but what would the husband say?

Daruma

imagining Bodhidharma's mind from Hokusai's sketch
of a lost portrait (1817)

The mind's open cage awaits its tiger
and no other. Who sets the fire will not
own it. No cure or prayer can break desire.
Go, live by proverbs, then tell hot
about cold and find nothing to say.

It is a summer's afternoon rain, incalculable,
as if no ground could take it. The water
sinks no more, and for a while the luster
of murk, the sequins of drops, the chance bubble
and swirl, announce beauty in a bleak day.

He begs who wishes to know God, and sings
who hopes God is deaf. Learn and forget
to earn not being forgotten. Guard everything
and lose the one thing. A field regrets
not drought but fence. Heat fathers hay.

A morning, let us say it was morning, or later
but not evening, but it could be true of night
for the dark knows it is coming and it is right
to dread time. In the morning, if the mind falters
it won't be clarity's fault. A poem is delay.

Count the seeds, the fruit and blossoms, but who
can count the roots, or count without them all?
Numbers prove because they haunt the truth.
A thousand warnings will not keep a single
secret. To rest well, know your way.

The racket only seemed to begin when he
first heard a new sentence of noises,
but even then its antiquity was obvious,
for interruption gave birth to the first story
by forcing its end. All lessons betray.

A lid for ears would love our minds; but blink
and lies elope with our world. Victory relies
on our skill with mirrors, to trap and sink
the enemy in his soul. Look into them but deny
nothing, unless you are your own adversary.

A landscape brings the sound of distant water,
and though we cannot see the source of the sound
we know this is no stream nearby, but rather
a cataract a mile away. How can sound
that is no echo tell its home is far away?

Never Tiger

For most artists it sufficed to throw a tiger
pelt on a house cat and claim the beast
of soul was captured in the silk of mind. The error
was so common as to resist the test
of facts, when tigers finally came to zoos
in Kyōto, Edo, and Ōsaka. Then the real
cat rose in rebellion against Truth's
contrivance. Still, those proffered rank ideal
burned through the tinder of vagrant hearts. The leap
was taken by the agèd Hokusai whose lion on a *fukusa*
is dragon spun, a portrait freed from deep
unraveled thought at its triumph ravenous.
He shuns those sleepy reeds where others stir.
An old youth might just this hunger master.

Hokusai, *Sparrow Dance* (1815)

Video producers have given Hokusai's sketches
their final resting place in vibrant dance.
The ancient figures caught in leaps and stretches,
donned wing sleeves and bowl hats

that cover their faces in every squat and pose.
Later, cheeks beaming, fans in hand,
they flutter to drumbeats and flutes, but those
are creatures of theatre—the compassed land

of sprung effect. Ritual ruminates to draw
the watchers in, for they need not
hoot and clap to be a part. All
communal life was dab, step, and note.

No video can take us to that solvent place
we seek in stage and clip but can't retrace.

Hiroshige, *Morning View at Nihonbashi Bridge*

opening image of *53 Stations of the Tōkaidō*, 1831–34

Predawn, I see my mother's reflection on the dark
TV screen. A night of turmoil. She'll think
it is evening when rising. A lord is upon us in stark
procession, crossing the bridge. His servants sink

from the weight they carry. The arch of wooden planks
creaks, and the fishmongers and dogs part to let
it pass. I too must bend, to salve her blanks
of memory, dispel visions and visitors she admits

might not be, in gulps, fearing her mind.
A gentle pilot cannot spare the waves
or what's in them. No more can the lord find
a cause to not disrupt the poor who crave

his struggle. He is an illusion as they to him.
A light opens, then quits. Morning, then?

Hiroshige, *Shinagawa*

1st station in *53 Stations of the Tōkaidō*, 1831–34

Sunrise on the great road to Constructivism.
Four catch-full ships approach;
another is moored, its rudder geometrism
dipping out of the bay. The women broach

their wares to the daimyō's retinue, in vain,
for though they've just begun their task antiquity
they will exit right behind a Cubist curtain
of houses and pines. The image gravity

finds the rudder, rectangles passing the lens
of a triangle, a card gambled on the blue felt
of visual thought. The coastal hive of dens
and shacks stack up like chips, for the day has dealt

and the struggle between flatness and the real
is on. Art wagers on the dual soul.

Hiroshige, *Kanagawa*

3rd station in *53 Stations of the Tōkaidō*, 1831–34

Abstraction is the eye's shorthand for suspension,
the holding off that other details may come
into the mind. But it is not an absolute,
as our moderns think when they execute
their spill, slice, and rub. At random
they proudly shove reference into oblivion.

Hiroshige grasped that the abstract forms of land
are clearly different from those of the sea, even
if the object in question is man-made.
A sail, a hull, take on geometry and shade
in ways unknown to field, in roofs unseen,
for it is the eye that paints and not the hand.

The grammars of city, ocean, sky and streams
train the mind in the freedom of their schemes.

Hiroshige, Ōiso

8th station in *53 Stations of the Tōkaidō*, 1831–34

Need, however natural, taxes our patience.
Our lord has planted trees to shade and feed
our path, hackberry and pine, but when the rains
come, the coverings and hats we wove from reeds

are no help. By bails and bundles we teach
our lives to mean; by steps our journeys mark
how we are spent on roads that never reach
their end. We enter them and depart

and we obey and trade, carry and disown
as if we too were spoiling cargo. We plot
our humble get-by. A meager village is home
for the storm, grateful warmth, a pot

with almost soup. So little is so much.
With two steps we know enough to judge.

Hiroshige, *Okabe*

21st station in *53 Stations of the Tōkaidō*, 1831–34

Only his travelers combine verticals and curves,
and two trees whose arcs a broken crown
might make. Otherwise, the roofs
angle and the channel wall slabs down.
The hills and waters breast the fragrant scene
which wax drip pines enclose.
Though not the measure, the prism of all that's seen
is the traveler, burden-bound and tenacious.
The dorsal weaves belly, the conical hat
rounds, the simplest cloths plane and bulge.
Reed synecdoches of forests trot
their human ambulation against the rush
of herded current. No shadows stain
this drama before, too soon, the promised rain.

Hiroshige, *Kanaya*

24th station in *53 Stations of the Tōkaidō*, 1831–34

A season tips its hand with cresting waters,
or so the travelers surmise, for what else
could explain the lack of a bridge across these tatters
that once a reeded bank so calmly pulsed?

From afar an artist watches the servants stripped,

flushed from struggle in winter thaw, their master
hoisted and his luggage too. They drop like shells
on the final sand, blank as if it were
a sea. Were these obedients not here to tell

the ground from open tide, our eyes, adrift

in distance would wager coast and fishing hamlet
and wonder in reckless poise how maps could get
it so wrong and be trusted still. A palette
minds the lost that currents soon forget.

Gates

after Hiroshige, *Tanokuchi Coast*, Yugasan Torii, 1853

They rise—by road, from water—to welcome one
world dying with the birth of another. Journey
duty, each step a present torn
up with its own now. A sudden torii
provides a bird, self-blind master
of path, a perch. Like arcs and portals of older
cultures, torii endure beyond meaning.
What gods, mobs, and conquerors loitering
now draw the tourist and the archeologist.
Torii that bloom, abandoned by temple or village,
in otherwise nature, forget which side's
the world and which the rampart of spirits,
though a pointed wind will change as it volleys,
knowing whence it came, why, and when.

Hiroshige, *Kyobashi Bridge and Bamboo Yards* (1857)

A pictograph of bridge, moon and merchant
caught Whistler's eye. We are drawn instead
to the presaged skyline of our time, the burdened
nets of rationed clouds, the hard-edged
rampart of vertical wealth that sheers Central
Park in many photos and films. Doubtful
Edo's bamboo stocks climbed our colossal
norm, yet the travelers on the aural
arc are likewise scaped by gray torrent.
The artist swells the view to shine the lone
boatsman's take of his unimportant
fate, and beckons dual perceptions by one
strangeness. Their path is what their view will mold.
Afloat, his mind becomes our world foretold.

Blanket Warmer

at an ICU

No rush like matter's panic before a void.
Off Naruto, Edo-period masters
Hokusai and Hiroshige beheld the roiled
expanse, in which fishermen saw disaster,

as emblems of their purifying compulsion.
Today a skybridge and tourist boats reduce
the scene to aberrant glance and profit function.
Unaware, the artists also prophesied

these coils of warming wools patients and kin
request amid the frigid pavilions. Like eyes
in vigil, the fingerprint swirls spin
in place, stacked, weapons loaded with the promise

of comfort. All around us, the treachery
of fraying from tubes, in bleats, caught in machine
fervors that cannot pull us from the frenzy
and vortex all flesh becomes. But clean

warmths mantle both the patient and
the sick, who shell here in numbing solace
like priests in long spent blanks and bones
with carnate stains, in failure's sure embrace.

Katsushika Ōi, *Night Scene in the Yoshiwara* (1850)

There are no secrets here, or that is all
there is. The light obeys, and from across
the street we are the girl whose shadows fall
on patrons and courtesans, all caged by laws

to district slavery. She and the garden of women
bristling with sun pins know the town's
grids and order. Though proscribed, fashion
reigns. Even the servants carrying lanterns

have a place above and beneath a place.
Sex too is theater, with script and audience.
The backlit geishas, robe and bulbous
hair, bass the rhythm of this transience.

A form must owe so much more to light
than color, for blocked it clarifies the art of sight.

Tsukioka Yoshitoshi, *Cooling off at Shijō*

from the series *One Hundred Aspects of the Moon*, 1885–92

Tempting to think it is enough to lunge
inward when the times crack and the demons stroll.
At center's edge the horizon is the plumb
line and muffled thunder plays the role

of whisper. Her angled head hangs midway
between a full moon and a lantern's drum,
and notes the arcs her phantom foot mislays
upon the waters. The moon, too, is done

with mirror's glow and seeks in echo the brethren
arc of moment's spin. A panic unfolds
in starfish wings upon the gray and crimson
gown, though in her a reasoned sadness holds.

Her hand sustains her on this final pier;
into the future a living past must peer.

The Mystery of Immediacy

on the poetics of Tadao Ando

There is an invisible fulcrum between cause and effect,
called architecture. Causality is enigma
for its host is intuition, not reason.
When approaching, in and through a building, reject
the model of the mind erected in wood or stone.
What seeks shelter is the moment, prismed magma,

current tamed. To think and be thought—pause,
its revenue and requisite. The skin of concrete shimmers
like water stolen from five in the afternoon.
The planes free and deny the path of loss
welcoming. One window in one space whispers
the sacred, unveils it as a whisper to those for whom

music is a forensic pleasure. Steps return
us to planes—the sun, thought's nocturne.

BELIEF

Syncretism

Lumped beliefs, like populations,
breed their panoplies. Soon
it's thankfully hard to tell
root from self, past from burden.
These Miami front-yard shrines
hallow fertile confusion.
Santa Bárbara is Changó in Cuba,
but in Brazil the god of thunder
is paired with Jerome. Metaphor
is always local. The belief
is the same, the mask cannot help
but fall away in the rasp of rapture.
Smoke, chant, fruit, and blood.
There are wisdoms oceanic,
and they too have a god,
Olokun, and a sultry goddess
Yemayá, crossing his unforgiving sea
to the New World made old
with prayers that reverse
the miner's toil and the smelter's
bullion. In fusion lies
the pearl, grime clumped
into a world, spun yet still,
the way Ochún sits knitting
at the bottom of the river,
patient as marriage.

Yemayá

Her followers have come to the sea,
to its flurried hem, to bring
the goddess their cosmetic tribute.
Baskets of white flowers
among which bristle mirrors and lipstick,
perfume bottles—the raucous fineries
of the temptress. She who also guards
over the serious chores of birth
and navigation, who rules the rocking tide
and its endless cradle, has borne
a thousand constellations
and called each star a god.

From her all the orishas came,
and the orisha in each flesh-closed
worshipper. She dances, though,
because she alone can grasp the music
in the thunderous herd of their chants.
For all her sway and milky mothering—
despite hips she sheathes in her fishtail
as her arms arc to coax the flower
from cobra shadows—
she is alone. Confusion reigns

over those who believe
that only the maternal nurtures
the vital surfaces of a punctual life.
The scientist who suddens onto a mold
hovering through his window, to land
on the petri dish of his worktable,
knows the distinct elation of ambushed
command. The sudden idea, which nestled
timeless in the common dark of daily life,
cracks forth from its oblivious shell

to tell of suns that hold the planets' array
or pry tragedy from ritual plays.

The gothic spire, the lace of sonnet,
the blush of personality in tempera
and oil, all were strummed from the dead
strings of chance because she taught
the self to listen for harmonies.
The surgeon masonries locked
without grime, the art of pouring stone
to homage the vault of sky, the cook's
iota that makes gunpowder out of rocks,
the disks that tame stellar distances,
the myths of compassion, the pagoda
and the steam engine, law and glamor,

all these she trembled from those
of her children who would not sleep
forever in the dank of unmapped stone.
Likewise her handiwork caught
the glint of mask, made face
the dramaturg. She alone defied
the tyranny of depth to make the deep
come live among us. Sullen wisdom
cocooned tongueless, soles unsullied,
left her a hungry world to hold in her arms.
Let Him anchor, She will sail. Let Him
scour the hiddenness for hushed heroics.

She blessed the leprous king
whose brow became a silver shield,
and the poet who could not mime away
his hearse of pleasures when, at last,
he came among his peers to praise his king.

The slave who yearly donned his master's
madness in silken revelry, the noble lady
whose golden cheek bought the fighter's flesh,
they too have learned from her that the soul's
harvest is open aired, freely visible,
and skulks only when brute denial fears it.
A mother only hides her hate, not her love.

Scarpia

Tosca

I too love the Church and kill
for it. You will never hear in me
the nervy mouse inside the stolen shrine,
but the swirl of the goblet where the laurels of the vine
contest for my approval. A toast to the free
who bow to native order and repel

invading liberators. There is no wrong
without right conditions. No right without
a debt to broken codes, the bent line.
Behold the valiant who hide like women behind
women, disguised, wheeled in fervent rout
from manly combat. From art and song

they've culled a fraud's license to dream tomorrow.
I am noon's pillar, stripped of shadow.

Scarpia (Aside)

Tosca

I heard those ripened, muted swoons, although
that was no kiss—a dagger sunk into my chest.
What use authority if it cannot impose
a hidden will? The songbird, let her muse
the painter in his cavern, his mettle at the test,
while she flickers here for me, beyond sorrow
and contrition. We are all caught between tides,
like urchins sprung or crabs denied a nook
from ravenous waves. She'll paint him a tale of flight
on a ship of words. I offer the blight
and bliss of wronged conviction, what the good book
prescribes for elevation. I am the night that hides
nothing, confesses the hunt, enables nature
purchase in the soul. To love is to endure.

Scarpia (a Cavaradossi)

Tosca

Behold, master of predictables, the moldy
loaves beside your sleeping head, which you
call art. Freedom is no flame, a smoky
ember at best. Conviction cannot brew
your tea or warm your bed. But I know
how the latter's wormed. You wrestle and pine
and hold stars ransom for the kiss she'll blow.
I live for the art of the hunt, a pursuit as fine
as clamorous dungeon summaries of fate, and one
which makes the latter possible. Uruk's king
could not command his flesh to rise from stubborn
dream, though you will shine the night to bring
ovations down. Brothel pity. I
guard the timeless grove while your paints dry.

Il Principe Ignoto

Turandot

What better way to become known by all
than to stay nameless? "Son of Heaven,
I ask to undergo the trial." Seems odd no one
inquired if the bold suitor was royal material.

In refugee garb, no guards or entourage.
Persistent, yes, and that heroic fire
the tough princess would mistake for desire
in the gongs of his eyes. But "she is a mirage,"

her ministers claim, "the head of a woman with a crown.
A hundred others await, and jewels to boot."
She is not the prize he is aiming at.
She will be the consort to his renown.

Yet he too must feel dismissed by the past,
strangers forsaking bitterness at long last.

Turandot non esiste

The rock doves' tribute to nothingness
is to vanish into stillness when a smear of gesture
jars the gearwork of feeding. Those terror
leaves behind harden, for in hunger largesse
is crassest luxury. For Husserl, consciousness
if always *of* something, so vainly empty
is the promise of void as immanent plenty
that the illusion of absence icons how life punishes.
That generous gift, that reverent turn of cheek
soon become the targets of contrition,
wishing one *had* betrayed, avenged, shunned.
There is no good that does not wound the meek
into repentance. The stabbed girl on the floor
soared with private joy once, and no more.

Dido to Solomon

In truth, of wisdom much nonsense is told.
A ruler must rely on baser forces
to see a path to clarity. We are builders
by instinct, founders by necessity,
and wisest when swept by love's brevity.
The greed for rage which our brothers
knew, cured us—enough that others sages
thought us from our calm. From youth we were old
and thus drawn to stone to outweigh time.
We passed over the spill of regnant crimes.
How surprised you too must have been
when barbarous flame abjured what we had built,
and we survive in words: a mythic queen
and a prescient king. Idols adorn your guilt
and a borrowed sword mine. In truth, we bowed
to lovers whom we took for Love, and sowed
our people's miseries, yet happy to be proud.

Solomon to Dido

I gathered lilies and queens, confusing them
with messengers. From my father, words; from mother,
deference. From both a tooth for beauty and an eye
for comfort. The real palace was the mind,
and the real hearth the pleasures I would find
in a harem of thoughts. In trials, I would try
my hand at theater—that scene in which terror
would prove a mother's love, sent by heaven
as any poem or statue. By paradox,
image, and epigram my mind wandered like a fox
in dove rookeries. My desires were mislaid
in the mystical, but how else to enamor the future?
Flesh prays by being flesh unafraid,
baring sin's memory and its wages in our nature.
Changes nothing: the drag of perfect hunger,
the tilt of the dancer's waist in windy flowers,
the antelope of shadow, the gnaw of stolen anger.

Leda to Mary

When it comes, my sister Danaë tells me,
power is sudden and brief, but the effect
possesses your life. The need, the curse of progeny
is a woman's battlefield, glory nebulous
as men's. Our wing-spread lord, tremulous
in strength, made me mother of beauty and loyalty,
ax and oracle, builder and burier. To reflect
what in the soul resides, and not the world debris,
is our call, but knowing is not obeying's
twin. Amid inevitables, we give in
but refuse to confuse love for earnest worship.
Those wings that heralded our fates
removed all whim and frivolous hope.
Your son, in whose being two natures mate
into a mystery, raises the litany of siblings
split by the grave into a novel kindling.
Let fires and stars rule instead of kings.

Mary to Leda

Only a woman's predicament changes history,
for swords and power molt their wielders often,
and the river courses on, blind to sea.
So is conscience—a single tide, in motion,
full—its attributes shape passion.
Where it takes us, there we are free,
so we know not "obey" like oxen,
nor "relent" like the net's take at the fishery.
We neither feed nor starve it, but become
its kind as it transforms us into its home.
What shelters from within, from the storm of the world
or the vice of mistaking want for need, is a gift
immortal. It carries our frailty and unfurls
the path of humble mission. What strength without it?
The wonder: what was asked of me was borne for me.
At the foot of death, tears were torn from me.
I serve by a light whose changes none foresee.

Helen to Bathsheba

I know your kind of sleep, like water over rocks.
To some, a glassy sparkle. To us, a constant
turmoil, a maze we are guzzled by
for life. When we dance or wash, our minds
must attend unseen lusts which find
us, laurel bound. This fate we try
to endure, makes us scorn our terse and fragrant
youth and yearn for sallow wisdom's knock.
At least, your kingdom stood, your son would reign.
No raft of love saved Andromache from the pain
of the widow's slaughter, the boy's plunge, the flames
that jawed her world. Your house, a prophet says,
will yield a master, virgin born, to tame
the power that preys upon our fragile days.
A spirit will shower his gold upon her drowsing.
A messenger, white with wings, will visit and sing
to her virtue, and she will be braver than the bulls of spring.

Bathsheba to Helen

What choices I had served only to undo me.
A soldier's wife too must follow orders
and strip herself of dreams that beg, procure
a stint in happiness. Beauty deadens pride.
We know ourselves absolved, can little hide
what enslaves us to our slaves. This blow we cure
by crafting sons into perfecting mirrors
which blunt, erase the slanders of blind time.
A queen alone is sovereign of her people's future,
and so she must outwit her impulse to be pure.
They killed for us, and so we are blamed for that,
but no magnet has a hilt or a blade.
No ewe impales herself to feed these dead
who peer from *klinē* and parapet.
But we, born masters of the flesh,
shielded but with silk, weave our mesh.
The careful fallen hunt at rest.

Homer to Moses

I, too, led them, in absentia,
standing back, in words, and letting the tale
and those it mauled burn off the misery
of the impetuous life. On the side of the enemy, scorning
the hero, I taught the little worth of trading
valor for victory. The gods, shrunken by treachery,
prove how death breeds bravery in mortals.
Except for the vain, I scribe without censure.
Your horde burned over thirty Troy's.
Who is the author of all they destroyed?
Who the Hector and Andromache of Ai,
the Hecuba of Jericho? Cassandra's
legion in Joshua's wake, in Horeb's sky
their white wail resounds. Your tablets flounder
on your history, commandments slain,
your lustful prince absolved but not Cain,
nor Lot's nameless wife, burned into stone.

Moses to Homer

Ours both are honor's ardent men,
and not those who prey on God's word.
A call is no license to disown
the reins on hilt that conscience and duty ordain.
That Joshua, he heard Him, too, proclaim
the right to mercy, yet he fell upon that town,
sparing that Helen and her gold, putting sword
and torch to the rest. I was the lone Sarpedon,
and like him glorified in order to be disobeyed.
That is why men are lost to ritual's feigned
purity which leaves them in appetite's brute cradle.
How Achaean flight was turned by the promise of rape,
and Trojan pride laureled by hoarding the apple's
bribe. Freedom's triumph is our take
on the gambled life—we can bet on Now
against Light, or push the servant's plough
in the bloodied field, alone, where few must follow.

Jonathan to Patroclus

The love of country is a manly task.
Not for nothing do we call it Fatherland,
and we his sons mirror him, for duty
commands we become whom we obey.
The old is not my king, for God may
choose paths for man and nation that darkly
meet our minds. But can the heart remand
what it desires? Is service but a mask?
Two passions can divide a man.
More, and he becomes an instrument,
and circumstance replaces will as storm
obscures the land it besieges. Battle weathers
thus, and in its howl and bleak, the torn
man earns the restful, promised altar.
A comrade love alone is clear and sure,
a light free of returns no doubt can capture.
That love is duty, too, a private armor.

Patroclus to Jonathan

Divinity, least of all, is loyal,
but a searing moment comes when all is risked
for purpose. Meaning is our distant home,
the reason, perhaps, we fancy banners and calls.
In battle's chaos we cling to the enemy's fall
as beacon, and gripe that in common life we roam
the leaden shore. Death's nearness has tricked
us into purpose; not so our gods of foible
and pride. This nursery of rants we beseech and bribe
pretend to shield and guide. We bunch in tribe
and honor, but only love unites and blesses.
I chose to join my cause, at last, and borrowed
the semblance of a hero, seeming thus to lesser
men the leader they hailed as they derided.
For the searing moment, I was the prismed shell,
another, even to myself, and well
disposed to honor whom I loved above all.

Kalypso to Paul of Tarsus

You might have, in your journeys, passed my little
island where mortal love buys endless life.
No faith required, though a warrior's back and knees
are. You think me a temptress, bully, and warden,
but my guest was too sad to savor the garden
into which fortune saved him, its perfumed trees,
its feasts for every sense. Such pleasures rife,
Ogygia invented the very concept of a blissful
soul life. This love you preach descends
from heaven, but already one of its citizens,
I felt it for him. Boundless, careless of response,
the goddess became a worshipper, the mortal a deity.
From time itself I offered respite, once
he forsook his ageing life and retook the alacrity
of his conquering past. But mourning will not rhyme
with loving. In his ark he sailed—a hard crime.
Only your words will live beyond your time.

Garden

The squirrels come, thin but by the dozen,
when my old mango tree is weary with fruit.
How does one rage against the urge to survive,
yet behold bitten fruit across the rotten
ground? As in battle, ruin becomes surfeit,

and only death is at ease. Blessed
are the sudden fungi for they have forsaken
the comfort of seed. Blessed are the fire ants
for they are not one. Blessed the abandoned
nests, who paid their debt. Blessed are the epiphytes

for they homage prophesy. Blessed the weeds
for they prove the folly of lineage. Blessed are the grasses
for they burn first or last. Blessed the spiders
who unwind their handless clocks. Blessed the dead
leaves for they rot like memory. The dark prize

alarms all into song. One for the nearing
hunter, others to mate or teach, another
to demarcate, yet none reflect
the wonderer who neither masters nor
restores and left so as to speak these things.

Barracks

Barns and prison bunks stole their style,
but who can tell originals from imitators anymore?
The times have us locked and ready. Cause
picks the pockets of our will, where we store
desire. Pawned for obedience, there is no cure,

no return. Freedom, too, abhors
apostasy. Blessed are the sergeants who trust
universal failure. Blessed the grunt for he
scolds the lack of pain. Blessed the tower
dwellers, sleeping the fat rolls of warm streets,

for their ingratitude medals the hero.
Blessed the arms manufacturer for science is his muse.
Blessed the deserters, the probate lawyers of inevitability.
Blessed the strategist, philosopher of blood, whose ruse
is tomorrow's poetics. Blessed the archivist of mortality,

the gravedigger, for he is the midwife of oblivion.
Blessed the flag waver for proving the brevity of pleasure.
A gaggle of orphans play out their rags
in the bombing footage, among gray ruins.
Their racket sirens no peace.

Resort

At the Buddha Inn everyone's alone and watching
for fire. The world is tinder. We knew these travelers
in a previous syllable of the infinite, but now we brush
past them. Grains of sand from a hand soon waving
to the children splashing, the dozing spouse trusting

your vigilance. Blessed is the servant, farthest from the confessor
and least punitive of men. Blessed the innkeeper,
farthest from the prophet and most cautious of men.
Blessed the cab driver, farthest from the convert
and bravest of men. Blessed the entertainer,

farthest from the saint and lover of the world.
Blessed is the tourist, farthest from the mystic and the most
awestruck. Blessed the guide, farthest from the priest
and the most compliant. Blessed the gardener, from
the angels the farthest and the most productive.

Blessed the lifeguard on his somber perch,
farthest from God and the most dutiful of men.
He cannot choose among those who call to him
for despair has masked them as one. He races to shun
both the salt of contrition and the fist of judgment.

Office

Like watch repairmen hunched over paper gears,
the workers phantom the small to annul the world.
They garner mind to task and deem task
all. Eyes lick the ant mounds of their roiling
screens; what one subtracts another adds.

Blessed are the diligent for ignorance cannot damn.
Blessed are the watchful for they presage the final heartbreak.
Blessed the overtimers for they've buried
the illusion of rest. Blessed the lazy for darkness
is shared. Blessed the bankers for they've heard

tomorrow's lies. Blessed are the secretaries
who confuse what they must. Blessed the accountants
who build our labyrinths. Blessed the lawyers
who spool our saving cord. A single certainty
lurks. Seen from the next tower, the latent

morgue of the vacuumed, lit office at night
files the morning's harvest of power. The worthy
field and raw mine, the furnace and the line
are ruled from these mires of the mild and torn.
The world condemns the polite ordering of the world.

The Lost Sermons of the Buddha

Devadatta

I too recall the life in which I was
his light and he my king. On the path
to the rising we danced inversely, and now I'm tasked
with needing the mastering pupil—no greater pain.
In this, our last life of night, I rein
my mind to scribe his sermons, and for me asked
nothing, at first. In secret, I brewed my wrath
and dutifully scrolled his words in the shade of his trust.
Even he forgot what I alone have stored
and therefore own. By service, I am authored.
His captured words, the bloom that will not rot
the stem. A wife abandoned owes herself
to a new master, so memory's hoard cares not
for origin but possession. The leader deserves
to be spared reasons. I set off to rule
who hope to flee the fate of rounding mule
and frantic moth. What flames life gifts to fools.

The Reef Sermon

Among mountains sowed with seashells
I came to rest from myself and entered the sea,
walked on its sand beneath a foam of stars,
and stood before its city of bones. Thunderous
with fish, inks, prisms, shaded by ravenous
fronds, pocked with crevices, like a mind far
alien yet mind. Grown from learned debris,
a hive of lives in forms that will not tell
themselves from where they lie, or if craft or chance
it was that let them seem the saving trance
of belonging. The city of bones ranges beyond
the eye's grip, rises to air past veils
of spores. Its thorn touch belies its horizon
scope which nearness cannot contain, like trails
we pace in lost now's. By nature built
to anchor flux, shelter the wheel, tilt
the sun. It owes to centuries, not man, its debt.

The Ash Sermon

The art fire bequeaths, numbing dust,
marries black and white to shut the book
of rainbow. Swept in air, washed, speaks
with earth. Deaf to touch, flees nose
and tongue, the fated sum of flesh, rose,
and hearth in uniform gray. End is meek.
No banner or stone, the winds its erasing brook.
Patient sign of urgent flame it trusts
to free. Formless, it clumps with fat that drips
from altar to make soap. In palm it slips
or lifts to cloud the memory of what it had been.
Shakes off from surfaces it will not taint, yet feeds
the field and once forest ground. Alien
ghost of seed's lurk and end, it pleads
our nothingness. Escapes into life
and from it as words from sighs and back—rife
with change yet timeless, must take what it must give.

The Cloud Sermon

Shapes infirm, hulks sight cannot touch,
They wither hover quick from similitude.
Even dark they harem our view, pliant
clumps in chaliced doze. Passing, they shroud
as do bulks that root or stalk the ground.
When the sky fills, they meld with kind, ignorant
of ownership. Exiled from altitude
to blank our paths, they succor earth and drench
our breath. In peaks alone, at times, they bow
to us to teach us clarities since shadow
is petal common. They herald spirit to the wise—
tireless vapor's toil, infinite in shape,
matrons of every season, indifferent to us
wanderers burdened with name. Like their shade,
we brief respite and grateful know our fullness
come to light. To rise we teach the harness
gold is mist, our trail blind to duress.

The Monsoon Sermon

Abundance, our enemy. Drowns way and traveler.
Torrent dreams of drought, as drought of torrent.
Need, the great baffler, confuses with bluntness.
The rain comes when and as it must,
the world's eyelid shut, thick as lust.
Conditions are sovereign in all but the free whose lightness
natures courage. Flesh, flesh is the mendicant.
The world's rush seeks the navigator
who is the melody of his meager raft,
born at last to need the freedom of his craft,
alone. Simpleton sky who dreams in pairs,
turns earth to sea with a vertical flood to palm
the mirror known and make it world's repair.
But world's three tongues alone can rightly calm
clarity to us. The craft, pilot, and river;
the three faces of time; sower, harvester,
and cook. Thought, word, and the silent knower.

The Edge Sermon

The soul of the moment, these plummet promises.
The path pretends it holds us until it ends
on one edge. The eagle has but one—
the ground. Seasons author their perfect limits.
The wheel is one edge whose tireless pivots
the axle will disown. What is a cliff but a torn
sky? We rampart from others, but what defends
us from pride? Forces are as forces
grip. The blizzard within, the private storm
break past human congress. No harm
is alien, no love natural. A line's fate
is to blur. Gate and door are marked by hinge
and man by the reach of his step, a tongue the gait
that utters him as first warmth spring.
Dire resonance, dear to the binding know,
your reins the last to give, penitent furrow.
Axle, the ninth spoke none foresaw.

The Memory Sermon

Can the story break from its calendar,
that nest of sighs and breath of fiery solace?
Trim sails bump with wind, needling
the tilting mast which, bound, cannot course.
Remembrance—cradle, anchor—stripped of dross,
is new gold in an old sea, reeling
then calm with unveiled stars and brevity's peace.
Memory scours dream's clay and mortar—
the fragrance of toys, the brush of sandy foam,
voices musick'd by loss, love's tome
scrolled away. No one can sow what's been
sown, regress fruit into stalk, abjure
the lessoned scar which roots now in then.
Easier to harvest distance when I ruled inured
to pity and a prophet came to melt my ear,
mazes prior—than weeks ago, that fear,
this sigh. No horizon is ours or near.

The Tool Sermon

Diligent as the plow, the moon returns, its cold
light the shadow of the sun. Hammer, pen,
ladle, blade—our creatures of use, extensions
of sense and flesh. Our moons, were we
their sun, but they are no mere
mirror, rather growth we lack, completions
which in turn unfrail our thin born
knots. From fire we feed and learn to mold
our poured metals. We furrow and hunt, ponder
how labors muscle, song voices, number
marks, symbol recalls. So each tool
and its greater issue define each person
by the task he becomes. But what of the pensive fool
who is his path, toil and tool but burden?
In chant he slowly flees from the daily flame,
defying defiance itself. Words cannot tame.
In mirrors he vanishes, eclipsed by the frame.

The Gifts Sermon

Who deserves the sun or has earned
the day, the perfect rain, or the curative night?
We are the fruit of givens which we dare
to own. A melody on crafted strings
is no bird in their cage. It also sings
on branch and eave. Talents and virtues we snare
with our names, into legacy take flight.
We but embers where once their glow did burn.
Valor, insight, mercy, language—all
by fated chance bequeathed, though they befall
the harkened servant. Who listens to the light
speaks and lives it. Who claims, betrays.
At last, we shall all escape, like sun's bright
music unraveling the fountain's muddled maze.
No names will find us safely then.
The origin of deeds and words will be their end.
No shadow will mark the haunts of men.

RES

Husserlian Meditation: Truck Tires

Beside me stalled in traffic, a white pickup
with four huge worn tires, powdered

in the flour of cement, their treads
a vanquished weave of hexagons

and crosses, ghosts an archeologist
could fathom into spoors, or a chemist

think murk's nascent crystals. I read
erosion, commoner, but I've seen

such blurs mean life, proof, and hope
to other learnings denied me. The lyric

elegist is grateful the light has turned
before he unhaunts, pretending free

in a world vapid grimy. I veer
into the pharmacy lot, and the truck

jolts on, its halo stocks in tow
heaving, galactic, as if awakening.

Husserlian Meditation: Torch Lighter

The palm-sized train wagons of boyhood
chugging the iron veins of course, also

did not know they were one thing and many
at once. The room as province, the crevice caves

and peek of forests that rim plastic geologies,
all dicta turning shelter into unsheltered

theater. A microcosm's synecdochic chant
echoes, too, the boy's frame, all heart,

with the engine dragging its entourage
the way our cardial furnace clocks our lives.

Through lungs that would be underbeds
and limbs that leg the woods of his life,

and minds of curtained glass whose glints confess
the world within and the one without owe

each other the trouble of reflection, the train
fulfills his colossal need for play. A thousand

journeys trace each other into destined alleyways
where the man still new to the real will decide

which ways to recover the thrill of a world contained
bring joy and which deliver him like cargo.

Husserlian Meditation: Ringtone

The choice muses on the broader circus of other
ears, for rare is the time when he alone

will hear the call. How will they turn in smiles
that applaud his duck quack phone or the heavy

metal of griped guitar? To show there is no sense
of show, he might pick the stock clicks and hoots,

the marimba or the classic ring of clunky phones.
What a choice says is never what it means,

as therapy confirms, so those he sought to put
at ease grasp now how deep the narcissist goes

to put them at ease. There is not, and never has been,
a private world, a self-reliance free from mock

and lure. This hive whispers to itself in chimes,
screens, and blurry thumbs. Each face ponders

the host in its cupped palms, unable to find
or lose, map or flee, to make a verb of life.

Husserlian Meditation: Thumb Drive

Not even thumb-sized anymore, the trope
has expired without leaving a denotation in place.

Amoeba Drive? Why Flash? Everything in a computer
splays the universal mind before the pin of brain.

A whale shark hovers agape through a sea
of fertilized snapper eggs, gorging tens of thousands

in a gulp. The shoal is undaunted, spilling
the milk of its future in numbers that humble

giant and single fish alike. Each snapper swirling
in the unraveling knot of its tribe was one

egg which, devoid of singulars, smoked the waters
with exponentials to outbid hunger and element.

The USB on my fingertip holds ten lives of thought,
a library, and prairies—wheel with no axle—waiting

to unstarve the ever hollow gut of tiny life.
A world in a carat-sized bleak stone

inside a plastic case. To the snapper, the whale shark
is a mobile Persia whose shadow leaves no room

for conquest. To the whale shark, the snappers' seed
is Kansas, a nest of horizons tireless in scroll.

Nothing outshines or outsizes the mind, hence
it is our model of God, cosmos, and doubt.

Husserlian Meditation: Remote

Were it the weapon it seems at first,
it would have only one or two options,

not a calculator horde of numbers, arrows
stabbing away from themselves like the sex

of magnets. The red circle with the white
circle inside it, a radius sticking out

from the perimeter—all this to say the sign
for Power—but in these initial entries

into the object's life in the mind, there can
be no presuppositions. So here, resting on palm

and fingertips, the remote is only far
from the TV and an extension of me,

the dove at the end of the day's deluge,
the compass bumping into a new world.

It points and teaches our hand to point,
hugged in the now boring magicals

of gadgets shooting our commands to other
gadgets. The system's slavery is never done.

On-off of old, channels and volume,
have become a library of submissions

to vapid will. The weapon metaphor might
have been preempted by a harmonica.

But tonight, stood up for the second time this week,
there is no music in the conjure. Only the slash

and vaporizing blast. A blur of channels
smears actors into digits of a shallow grave.

Husserlian Meditation: Barcode

Viral kinesis, a haunting of rhythms
that seem, like rain, unthought

yet bloom into novels with the scanner gun.
Is a life contained a life betrayed?

Suspicion rears when the reading secrets
its language. Things tattooed with archive,

as movie killers with barcodes on the back
of their heads. The young at times

don the code for Code, the sign for those
who mock the chicken-factory numerics

of market-life. Double irony: by affirming,
the code denies; by denying, it embraces

the rumbling informed subsistence.
I've succumbed, scraping barcodes from

medicine vials less scavengers steal what I
no longer have, admittedly: an identity.

I am a set of planned breaches. Ladders climb
the crumbling castle wall. Self as surrender.

Cage the vain aesthete who thinks to defang
the vulgate menace. Self as prisoner.

Burn the bureaucrat who promises ease
with each lashing of progress. Self as lure.

Abandon the pleated confessor who metes the wages of sin
on the backs of minted men. Self as punishment.

But all this buffets the delicacy, the marvel of sign
harped with strokes whose slightest variant

reminds that utterance shoals into myriad forms
to remain a shoal. Meaning cannot be selfless.

Husserlian Meditation: Sunday Rain

Front stalled in invisible ranges,
the maths of which we cannot see but drench.

Mere rain, when others but a few hours drive north
are encased in undeniable failings.

My yard never turns the page on green;
even my weeds are lush. I go on pulling rounds

every now and then, when the fertile evils
bore the day and only symbolic real uprootings

of what should and must not have a say
fill the gut of soul with the silence of a filled belly.

As if ravenous I were harvesting, as if the years
of fat cows had ended and it is time to bring in

sullen bails into bolted quarters. But today
the rain has thrown the lock on warm doors

and left me to spy unwanted hoping.
I will rest or my day be just, my purpose

aided by the wise, my words taken as they're spoken.
The vengeful tired will be the gardeners of Paradise.

Husserlian Meditation: Expiration Dates

It's a guess, a date to stave off litigants
and trick consumers into discarding

what may still be fresh and potent. Pills
throwing in the towel, sauces refusing

overtime, even water decidedly showing its age
in its tight bottles. Our finales, to the minute

the Good Book says, are stamped on our souls,
yet we loiter and amble on shelves daily

and long-game alike, convinced the shadow
we don't see cannot find us. Not so much

as a heads up, a week to prepare.
The crash grind grip stroke bullet,

the virus Protean and the tumor searching for a myth.
The means may vary, but life, the spiritual tell us,

has a pull order on file. And likewise products hide
their range. Profiteers should want a bolder

display, a stamp heroic, an edict glow.
These peaches will die on the morning of June 6th,

and this ointment will rot the following 11th of August.
But one must turn the product, or squint into embossed

grooves, angle the edge a perfect angle, hope
a bump hasn't smudged the tiny red perditions.

Difficulty betokens validity. Nothing untroubled found
cherishes the finder, so when you exhume the date

from the busy label, you sigh it is not yours. What
odds that you and your canned peaches will die in unison?

CT Scan

You, the bent arrow
in the instrument that hums
the circle's taut bow.

You it hears with light
singing deaf, a broken drum,
the siren you fight.

Proteus

In the dream, the man is bathing
a large dog whose breed changes
as the chore unfolds, starting
with a rottweiler, then bulldog, great dane. . . .
Starts on the lawn, then shifts to the groomer's,
the man's bathtub, a creek from his childhood. . . .
First it was a dog he owns, then a former pet,
then a friend's, a dog from a commercial. . . .
It is as if the dream announced
this thing, then that, then changed its mind,
and it is then that the man understands
he cannot truly embrace the idea
that the dream has a mind to make up
or change, for then life would have
a toolbox, a menu, program tabs, training schedule. . . .
hence throwing into the acid of questions
whether *he* has such powers—to alter,
navigate, reflect, cure, develop. . . .
this tumble of paradigms, themselves
becoming a chain, sequence, sentence, syntax,
metonymy. . . . because the *thing*
—the announcement—
cannot simply be a fate but a motion,
a variance, an effect that churns the weather
of effects, topples the still life on the table
just when the painter had caught the just-so light,
right before the supper, the sole ingestion
point of the thing, the call to itself,
begins and leaves
everything else
twirling.

Swimming Pigs

Exuma, Bahamas

My students are in love with swimming pigs
they've seen online in their virals. Sleek,
and thanks to the glassy bay, they never reek
nor wallow in mud. Dumped in these tropic
unnaturals, they roam but were reported
dead. Tourists come to them. They shower
hugs, as if ever casually and everywhere
the world frolicked fattened prey into pets.
Behold how the dismissal of habits is enacted
with a goggled splash, lotion, and neon flippers.
No one accuses. Nothing but light is refracted
into the misty ledgers. The pigs' retort is deeper
than sea and history. They fire up the right
conversion with beauty at the helm of appetite.

Manta

Then, when I was six,
she took me to the *Aquario*
to see again the huge manta
whose eventual captive death
she would hide from me,
so fascinated, so in love
with the clasped wave night
of the ventral moon was I.

She'd say the keepers
had set the manta free
to be with her kin again,
her ache of children,
so I'd too want her
to be free of the pool
she marked relentless
with her path, herself
the rock she must roll
up the hill of the sea.

So that now, 46 years later
in the Emergency Room
of her seventh stroke, I'd
harbor a parched prayer
that my grandmother,
who set Havana's manta free,
might find that blue
that turns the dark
and shines
belly white
with joy.

Shutter Fauna

The coming hurricane has steeled our windows,
and behind them we hoard vitals and wait.

Young citizen frogs appear like decals
on the panes, the shutters vaulting behind them,

a too stern curtain for their foraging theatrics.
In normal weather they do not cling to the glass

for these residential hours, but now the light
that tides and nets the wings they devour

comes from inside. Where needs eddy,
there the mind takes the body, calm commanded.

The very model of obedience. Infants shock
to see a toy, fallen out of reach, refuse the order

to return that a hand has taught them familiar.
And they must learn that the bitten wrist

feels not at all like the ring, gummy and dead.
The frogs, now three partitioning the picture window

and harvesting the moths that cannot figure how a moon
has tucked itself into a bulb in a room shelled

by a zinc sky, or how the streetlight or the porch's
amber that never welcomed them, has sunk into such

strange thinness. And as the moths knew to seek,
so their killers knew. I get to watch them from below,

their pleated grip, the geared heart of tiny bagpipes
slick and big-eyed. I sat in the earth deity's chair

to watch fake heavens cage a meticulous massacre.
I know how this ends, as the infant will finally guess

there are things his flesh will master alone.
The imbalances of patience—that came to me like wings

or trusted legs, three days ago beside a dying woman's bed,
her eyes blanked by stroke, her breathing ardent with ending.

I called to her as she left me in a leaden space
that closed upon us—freeing one, keeping the other.

(for Regina Llosa, 1905–2005)

Oneiromancy

The dream of the hummingbird
insults tired sleep,
its clamp on flesh
like a wrench paying homage
to the crocodile. The flutter
in whose oyster of blurs
a double sphere
articulates fog.
Too geisha to elicit
the condemnation
of nightmare,
the hummingbird, alone,
succulent to the eye
and dripping in honeys
we could not suspect,
swings like the ax of horror
across expectation.
That is its crime:
only beauty rebels.

Tortoise Shell

Chalice of rain when it rains, and bowl of howls
in drought, and of wind's sand and cobweb.

Jeweled by the concave arteries of ants
and flicked by lizard tails like tongues in a skull.

Tipped by the brush of storm or leg, or dizzied
by what fell into this accidental trap, or a branch—

so that home and measure are one with prison
and tomb. So it was when the shielded master

keeled and could never right and slowly,
though in closing fits no doubt, perished,

and was scavenged and rotted, and finally
this dense mirror is left, erratic horn, blinding lid.

Snake

No other thing confines itself to endless
forms of a single form. Can fold itself

into flower or fist, unbraid into a line
that electrifies the sky it makes of land,
a bolt that stayed in matter and grew a spine.

Alone, in a nest of its sinuous kind,
or locked in the briny helix of mating's
fray, it frightens even those whose hand
copies five-fold the gift of longitude.

Despite the seeming regimen of grip or touch,
the medusa of tendril digit vine and talon
apes the legless reptile of the ground,

reminding us who pluck the curious fruit
what separates origin from similitude

is but a brush with chance.

Hurricane Warning

I must break her web to reach my hope
of saving orchids from the nearing storm.
Her perfect labors are doomed to punctual harm,
so I fret little, reasoning scope
and tally forgive erasing what I long
admired. The cattleyas saved, the frail rare
will hog into sleep while trees and birds share
a deluge of nakedness. Nothing common or wrong
about the spider's opal sail to condemn
it or the need to condemn it, for what must
will die. Obedience is mercy dark, a lust
to hush desire. Who is this old man
in the windowpane turned to mirror by shutters,
his webs of purpose torn by chance and others?

Feeder

The morning ritual, 7:30 sharp, seeds falling
black from my hands onto the concrete slab.
They will come almost immediately, hardly
have I turned my back on the oil-rich morsels
or the crackers I toss across the lawn,
for not all birds devour the seeds. The blackbirds
prefer the crackers, the cardinals the seeds,
the pigeons and blue jays eat anything.
I retire behind the sliding glass door
and watch them eat as I eat breakfast,
enjoying the parallels our natures breed
in us, acted out each morning.

They know me. By 8 they'll be perched
on the patio chairs or hopping on the floor,
their form of prayer. "We are hungry
and you're always on time. What gives?"
The squirrels come later, as if courteously
allowing those for whom the table was set
to have their fill. The crumbs, as it were,
for the little mammals, but there is abundance
for all, the intended and the opportune alike.
And bugs for protein, nectar for the hummers.
Plenty for those who believed there would be
and for those, just as hungry, who stumbled upon it.

Dreamers

It is not the doves I want to descend
on the seeds I throw out every morning,
but the cardinals and maybe the blue jays.
I like the blackbirds, too, walking like men
to a fight. I can tolerate, at times, the chirping
hopping sparrows if there aren't too many
of them. But the doves come in droves
and eat everything before the others have
a chance. Beyond gluttony, it is blasphemy
for innocence to hog, to put feast before necessity.
In their skulking porcelain, one can clearly
see power nesting in their brains, fiercely
clinging to itself, a nest that shirks the egg.
From the predator's peace, what can resurrect?

Puddle

My student sees filth everywhere,
Even in this dank, rotten-leafed,
cigarette-butt poisoned
tongue of late morning bronze.

It laces the oak branches
above it and folds the midday sky
in green convections.

Allow me to introduce you
to squalor's gorgeous mirror
who taught the golden youth
to catch himself in love.

This silent bed whose many sheets
are one mellifluous of shade,
has hosted boot and quandary,
astronomy and betrayal.

I cannot hold it accountable
for accuracy or permanence.
Surely it knew from the start
how short the mission
and how stark the light.

But linger, pupil,
where an eye might brave
the trough whose vapid depth
dared frame the trees, their sky.

Nocturne

Blue, the infinite within a boundary hue.
Edo artists relished its blood-drain
of sea dawns. Westerners learned to brew
from the Virgin's mantle the brim celestial stain.

Between the coloring book and the sky pots
wedging tombstones, it invades the otherwise
green. Few flowers: forget-me-nots,
plumbago, iris, hydrangea, gentians rise

to approximate themselves in the pressed pigments.
In the war against death, blue guards the pass
between hopeless peaks. Dim stream regiments
march in the mind sky of refracted masks.

It is blue that imagines green is born to die.
Sweeping for the dream sunk, a beacon's eye.

GENIUS LOCI

Call

Hotel Milvia, San José, Costa Rica

The last vendor's cry in Latin America
moves east behind the thick hedge—
el aguacaté verde, el aguacaté—
shifting the accent from the proper *ca*
to the final *té* to give his sung pitch
a foot as much in music as in language.
His shuffling soles provide a jazzy curtain
to his errant refrain, and then of a sudden
he stops. It seems a buyer has approached,
but this cause the quiet must surmise,
as with art whose maker's bent we theorize
from our confines, our sense of self projected.
Could pause alone be art's intent, the way
leaves desire to leave their hearts in gray?

Paraíso, Summer

Hotel Milvia, San José, Costa Rica

What sun the mango's shade permits is marked
by nouveau grasses and minute liriopes
beside a path moon-thick with gravel
and pocked rocks that balance the natural
with the placed. The very code of captured peace
denies liberty its full wing, rejects
the trunk's embrace of bolt or spring, of all
which presence, as if clocked by destiny,
bequeaths to an inflicted life. The fulcrum's call
blunts as well the compass stab of design
to favor wind that sways the ginger stalks
and eddies mutely around the measured rocks.
The middle's icon here is the passiflora vine,
abloom without choking, rampant but serene.

Flâneur

Caught in curiosity's web, he dandies mildly
in the cafés and boulevards of the nineteenth century.
Like a learnèd finger skimming the pages of the city,
he will linger and jot, stroll on, and fondly

hoard his catch of thoughts to his studio and work
them into works. Not all were artists, and like today
many thrill to seem it and don the gray
of mind's vocation. The ailing doctor, the thinker

of blurts, the stroller has returned to claim our age.
In biennials choked with thoughtless conceptuals,
they've risen to easy prominence. Erstwhile marginals
who mastered the humility of the gaze are now a scourge

of cleverness. Millions ape them on their phones
and laptops, scouring the nothingness that is their own.

Nessun dorma

The man in his fifties sits at the picnic table
asleep, his back to the wall of the building where music
is taught. I've seen him before. He is here to pick
up his son, a talented high schooler capable

of college rigors. He is dozing, or simply shut
his eyes against the summer that is fall
in Miami. I imagine him taking the toll
of his life, the pride in his son against the lot

of those universal anchors of pain and retreat.
But we cannot know for he is no prince
in aria before dawn, on stage frantic
to expunge soul with purpose. The mysteries we read

are puppets we make of ourselves. The cave is dark—
so we turn it into projection's fertile ark.

Echo

When the young die, for weeks they appear
in halls and crowds—the slap whisper of semblance
in a body or head, a gait, any remembrance
that likens death to life. It is always clear
that they are not, yet for an instant are
the one love could not guard or keep.
No ambition of need, no meticulous desire
could stay the crush or shot, the end's grip
on an unfinished tale. They walk toward us
as strangers, for in their world there is no
recognition of the living, even though
it is the living we see and not those
we yearn for. Projection, like love, is confusion.
It confesses feelings come home in reflection.

The Last Quarter of the 20th Century
in Miami

To watch them die, the heretic minds who fathered
mine, and to find myself as old as they
when, young, I searched and planted the seed
of this morning's summation. I'd hear them say
mundanities which, from them, fed
with bodied lives the glass harp and drum
of their works within me. Poems and paintings freed
exile from the panic and funeral of home
and claimed me with a history of art—alive
in the turpentine and the music of pages, the foreseen
present that hails and sunders. Before me
they breathed a brokenness from which I derive
still the maze and the string, both mine.
The wound bequeaths maps. From ruin, design.

View from My Mother's Last Hospital Room

Nothing but sky and the silver baroque
of air conditioners that hive the roof
of the parallel wing. Sloppy metallic
coatings thick with moon in the loose

sun, molten mirrors. Boxed
diligent organisms, mute
from this room they cool. Locked
in a bed by her stuttering heart, moot

all joys and bound to all
miseries, my mother hums in
and out of consequence. Stalled
from death by finer drugs, ruin

is destiny. She dangles a blank peer
at a deaf and frigid train churning near.

Eres débil

Before her son's dread of surgery tomorrow,
the ill mother scolds: "You are weak.
Look how sure I am, always," low
but steady, a whispered order against the meek

surrender to damp, clenched prayer, its void
hummed down by life. Neither grief
nor beggary can outweigh her rousing, joyed
possession of his obedience. His felt if brief

goodbye picked up its golden armor, for strength
invents the mess of story and the final field.
It expects embezzling memory to fix a death
and plop it upon the crafted, handsome shield.

She would recover. When a year later
she died, he took it mellow, soldierly.

Soon

"For each man alike is oppressed by his own trouble, but the
heart recovers quickly from someone else's grief."
  —Pindar, *Nemean Ode*, 1

A dozen years—one for each tribe,
month, apostle—are minutes for the wounded lost.
No Joseph triumphed, no chalice buried in the crib.
A blurring in life's sandstorm, at best.
In his father's arms when I last saw him, three
days before he was forgotten in a hot car.
A prism of promise, alert, strong, and free
from the premonition I hushed. Now a scar
in a family's weight of life, he grows in dreamt
stages: a vane of puberty at present, soon
a man stormed by lust, a completion confirmed
by necessary fiction. In the novel in which he blooms,
he will find his path, study and become.
He'll weep by his parents' graves when their time comes.

Key Largo, Nightfall

Beneath the sloth sweep of cerulean doves,
the thrown anchors of pelicans, and gulls nervous
proud, native to anger appetites,
I watch the last hour of daylight's
damascene of copper fronds the tide has etched
on our canal. The place and its catch
of scents—the sea is but 200 feet
to the south—simmer lost memories replete
with the home my child played innocent
of promised loss and my adult misspent
in ambition's pleasures. But I am old now
and accounting is my muse, when how
is when and where is why, and summary
nets a season's clarity. My cradle city
derided by history returns in smells and tastes,
where my sister taught me to speak and exile fates
turned like a coming storm. Our hands received
caterpillars from oleanders we believed
we had tricked to wander there, so natural
their passage from home to flesh. Time's feral
moments prophet those slight creatures
which we set down on the proper leaves to nurture
their ways through change. Sixty years later
I shed my silken cage by dark water.

Cognate, Port Largo

A sculpture pretending it's a boat slips
beneath my balcony. *No Compromises*
sails up-channel as a gull's cry dips
to angel its arrival. Sharply the prow rises
crowned with a steel anchor, a lone pilot,
four motors, 50 feet of white
and chrome, the lace fan of its wake lit
by morning. A swan could lock its grieving right
eclipsed by the yacht's invincible sword and mission.
No bow to icon, no promise to relent,
it breaks the word. In Spanish, *compromiso*
means "obligation." No bargaining, no duty bent.
Then, as the swan shudders to claim the air,
art, having no past, admits no heir.

Cytokine Storm, the Croc in Plague Time

Sequestered, on my balcony, I glance an odd
lump in the channel. Floats slower than the tide,
turning to scan perhaps, then it stops.
A hunter's calm, I think, in which it hides.
Then it lurks forward with intent.
I hurl a cigar butt to see it hook
the splash. It turns like thought, again.
Yesterday a manatee neared a neighbor's dock
and guzzled water from a hose for an hour,
a six-foot prey, lotus drunk.
How innocent it seems in its golden shower
now that I know how the water can darken.
At dock's edge I tempt a view of death
but see a boatman's Dodger's cap instead.

Car Wash, Key Largo

2 Samuel 14:14

The soapy drench is physics drawn to river
toward me, 15 feet away in my flimsy
chair. At first its body fans to deliver
brims to concrete sinks I had not glimpsed,
then narrows to speed unveiling dips and bellies,
then courses on to a hole with a remnant pool
anchored by a cigar butt. A halt belies
its reaches. A lump has pushed the gray drool
around the promised lake in delta featherings
while another drive has passed beneath my seat
to rest in my colossal shadow, clearing
its slate of suds. The flow now ponds in the heat
and readies its ghost mirror to catch me, gray
in noon's appraisals, the reaper of the day.

Fleeing Actium

New Year's, Port Largo

for Robert Nazarene

Summer on the backs of winter sirens the rich.
By late morning the canal regains its calm
after yachts and jet skis have shed
their docks for the Gulfstream. From shore
the festive clusters, wreathed in beer, ignore
our witness and the sunken life for pleasure's bread.
Banners stroke the distant sand where helms
brace against the sky, a melding in which
three dozen craft engage into a form.
What golden day can truly presage storm,
this nest of noise in a cell's blind horizon?
Naxos before the courtship and slaughtered maze,
when no Before held sway over the known
and Now no Pharos yearned in ledger's trace.
By 5, with hungers shorn, a flybridge boat
heads east and pulls a raft in tow.
The rising tide reclaims by ancient rote.

Balcony, Truman Street, Key West

POSH: Port Out, Starboard Home

Some prophet of triteness imagined luxury thus,
but soon the anagram became an adjective,
or a semanticized sound: a fluffy cushion's lust
to shield us. Even asses must hover to live
ideally. On my Truman balcony I watch
Conchers pass, masked for plague although
alone on near empty streets. They march
or ride bikes, their gait patient and thorough
on the en-soi promenade. Shutters and quiet
have calmed their famous boister into pews.
Masks to hoard illness become blighted
ritual; cotton armor pretends a new
civility. Corona's face crown gags a runner
angling for a stroke. Death is a task for the loner.

Behind him an 18-wheeler roars past,
black but for a stretch white space shuttle—
"Spirit of America"—starboard, gleaming its last
dash home. Our millennia have been marked by struggles
with disease, and we never ceased to build and grow.
In the gothic shade of aqueducts we outspent
all the muses could give us from their grove,
epic lutes, philosophies in paint.
We hunted death and measured silent stars.
In marathons of falling youths, progress outran
the racers. No wound, no pox could leave its scars
on our ambition. The Truman Street strongman
resumes his pace, fists pummeling the air,
a victory masque, though no one else is there.

Aubade

The midmorning light feeds my words,
a vice I got from painters great and poor
who labor in a rabbled mess, whose works
crowd my walls. They taught my eye to pour
details from the common rummage of bungled names
which sprang from a maker's moment and now dissolve
in daily fray. This light forbids the vain
ponderance, raises the crevice from the blunt of gloved
quotidians to stand disrobed in the solar mind.
The pool's motioned lace, the orchid's lobe,
the squirrel tail's refrain that curves to rhyme
its jolts. Morning welcomes the mind's grope
of all it becomes. This throng of world can hope
to choir when function is silenced by verdant trope.

Homage to Telesilla of Argos (fl. 500 bce), Port Largo

philêlias, hymn to Apollo; *oupingoi*, hymn to Artemis

A week away from the sea and my canal,
and the house repairs across the way are done.
In the house next to that one, with the banal
tuna on the canal-side wall, the garden
has been worked, the golden palms shorn
of frazzle and ripe coconuts, the tiki varnished.
I glimpse the gleam of new paint on the worn
hoisted hulls, the buoys tied and bleached.
The teak dining set honeyed by stain
has shed the silver weather had inscribed.
Fall's the proper time—cool, less rain—
to ready homes for visits from the tribe
of cast familiars, to revel in calendar's end,
although here all year one season reigns.

Behold how the copters spraying for mosquitoes cross
Largo in bands, south to north, their gray
plumes floating west in the winds that toss
fronds into waves. And although the bright day
is ideal for sailing, all the boats are still,
and the only motors I hear are overhead.
Shoals which travel currents to follow krill
let the fishermen sleep. The ocean's herds
have set their clocks. Hunter and prey hear
what each must to cue their urgency.
For none that live are starved of fear,
and none can drown time's poison melody.
The goddess sings to call her golden hind,
the silver tarpon, and the bronze hawk to mind.

Epistemology at Aleida's Swimming Pool

A world is no less itself when upside down
reflected in the pool, as if dangled from its heels
like a prisoner already confessing his innocence
or his guilt by his journey through condition.
A slight breeze ripples the water into rungs
the eye climbs across the harped semblance,
toward the point where image spills from the real
onto the trembling surface and there resounds.
Hearing and sight teach each other, mold
from wave and shot what we call World.
Yet mystery. Precision. The distance we know
by reverb and frequency the eye translates into size.
So the ear, too, has a vanishing point it borrows,
as shadow is courted into depth by aural eyes.
All else we touch, smell, and taste in nearness,
as if the body staked its right as nest
and center where horizons siren their numbers to rest.

Al Andalus

In courtyards of sun and night I find
my moment's calendar. Centuries, in a bud still,
bloom in the timeless mind as light pools
in the oyster palm of fountain to settle into motion.
Language—contained infinite—turns the rotation
of the moon into emblem, its one face spools
myriad yet same. A syntax of shadows fills
the atrium, the square Roman heart which lined
Bath and Córdoba, Byzantium and Havana and speaks
form into the form of mind. There rest breaks
the bread of words into tone, doubt, and palate.
The moon on earth—these walls cratered with flowers.
A blank that shines by night is an eloquent slate.
Each prayer a column; each column a blessèd tower.
Among lions I walk, and beneath the petaled combs
I am hovered from rivulet and harem to amber domes.
The wanderer's journey is the history of home.

Window on the Sea

Condado, San Juan, Puerto Rico

Sitting on a cement battlement (circa 1942)
where American turrets once spy-glassed
for periscopes, I join the sun-red tourists
coupled in their morning dallies
across an engineer's jetty of plopped boulders.
The sea hits the rocks with the huff
of popped-open grocery bags,
parodies of distant gunfire brought home
to muffled ears. The coral chunks
and concrete rubble long ago settled
into their guardian chore so that crab
and mollusk and the green blushes
each wave jostles then combs
accept these hulks as home.
It must be so, when each wave lashes
what it feeds, spilling kegs of livid foam
through caverns fashioned by how each trunk
of crane-dropped slabs has lodged
into community. The water rushes
the canyons, platforms, windows and ramps.
The take on all this, ten feet above,
is that of artifice still. Blunt need attained,
the drive to colonize makes nature.
The salt perfume and the knitting picks
of a hurried crab amid the silvered
leaves and shells and the varnished planes
proclaim that what's been abandoned
to the living cauldron
will be redressed.

Designated Smoking Area

Doubletree Hilton, Claremont, California
for Enrico and Nivia

"The tongue is ablaze"
—Buddha, *Fire Sermon*

How they climb, these fools of trees, ringing
matter, spinning toils of fronds to choke
the miser sun. How they've managed to bring
the vortex into themselves, to swallow hole,
dire wombs, the mercenary life, the thumbprint
maze we share. Lost though rooted, they spread
as we along the barbarous ways sprint,
amber hushed. Water and soil their bread,
the fire they steal from each other makes titans of weeds.
Yesterday, before Orozco's mural of Prometheus,
I saw humanity ablaze, not freed.
The forger spirit unleashed, need rises.
What brethren anchor can we hope to hold
in fire's stubborn world we embers mold?

Night Garden

The laughter of strangers makes them familiar,
for in groups of friends we all rise and burst,
then settle into talk that rattles up in intervals
only to glide back. As if all gatherings
were orchestras reading from the score of need and release
and played under the mute direction of an invisible
astuteness. All cultures in laughter are one.
My backyard neighbor whom I rarely see
has eight guests, and knowing nothing
but their mirth has rid us of this good fence
and distance. I ride their ritual, alone among
my dry trees and orchids, watering them
in the mantling dark. Normally, I'd head
inside by now, but with their nearness
and music kinship, I linger in their safety
and smile back to mind remembrances.
The lilies and bromeliads, the pelican flower,
the passiflora, mango, jasmine and mamey
soak up the unexpected rain I've brought
and laughter make of glistening leaf and fragrance.